MAKE it WORK!

SHIPS

Andrew Haslam

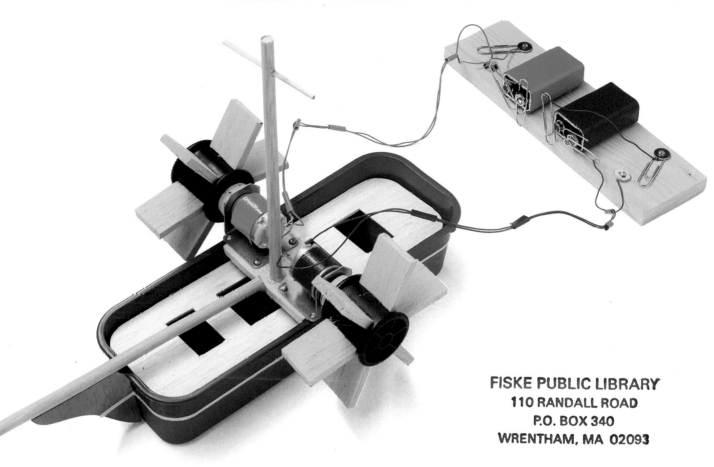

written by
Andrew Solway

Consultant: Simon Stephens
Curator at the National Maritime Museum,
Greenwich, London

WORLD BOOK / TWO-CAN

MAKE it WORK!
Other titles

Body
Building
Dinosaurs
Earth
Electricity
Flight
Insects
Machines
Photography
Plants
Sound
Space
Time

First published in the United States in 1996 by
World Book Inc.
525 W. Monroe
20th Floor
Chicago
IL USA 60661
in association with Two-Can Publishing Ltd.

**For information on other World Book products,
call 1-800-255-1750, x 2238.**

ISBN: 0-7166-1734-X (pbk.)
ISBN: 0-7166-1733-1 (hbk.)
LC: 96-60454

Printed in Hong Kong

1 2 3 4 5 6 7 8 9 10 99 98 97 96

Text: Andrew Solway
Editor: Francesca Baines
Senior Designer: Lisa Nutt
Managing Designer: Helen McDonagh
Project Editor: Kate Graham
Managing Editor: Christine Morley
Managing Art Director: Carole Orbell
Production: Joya Bart-Plange
Photography: John Englefield

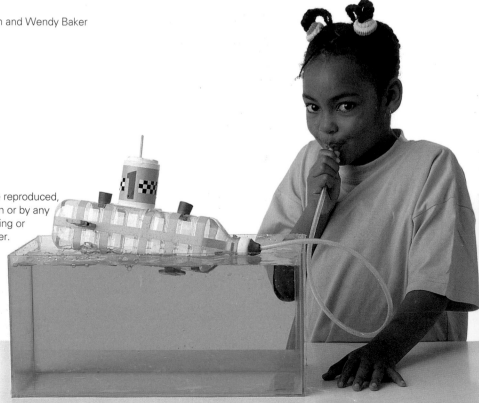

Contents

Words marked in **bold** in the
text are explained in the glossary.

Being a Shipbuilder

People have been building boats and ships for over 6,000 years, and today you will find a huge variety of designs on the waters of the world. While some have hardly changed over the years, there are also many incredible new machines, from huge aircraft carriers, to motorboats so fast they almost leave the water.

MAKE it WORK!
By doing the projects in this book, you will learn the principles behind even the most complex ship designs. You will also build a whole range of exciting models, from early rafts to modern working ships.

You will need
The materials you will need to make the models in this book—balsa wood, electric motors, propellers, eyelets, brass strips, glue, paints—are inexpensive and can be found in craft or model shops. You will also need some tools. All the tools shown below will help you with your shipbuilding.

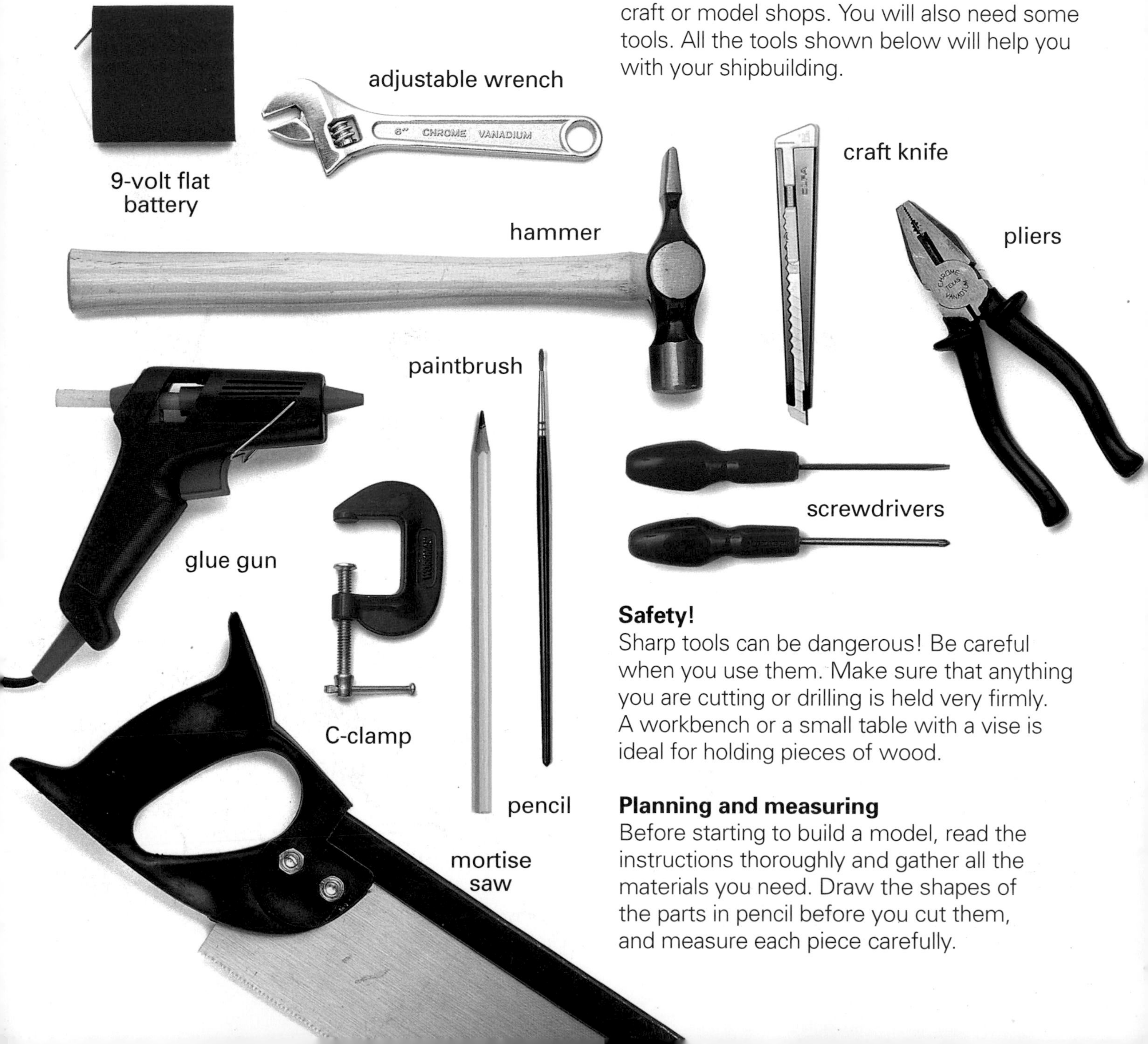
9-volt flat battery
adjustable wrench
6" CHROME VANADIUM
hammer
craft knife
pliers
paintbrush
glue gun
screwdrivers
C-clamp
pencil
mortise saw

Safety!
Sharp tools can be dangerous! Be careful when you use them. Make sure that anything you are cutting or drilling is held very firmly. A workbench or a small table with a vise is ideal for holding pieces of wood.

Planning and measuring
Before starting to build a model, read the instructions thoroughly and gather all the materials you need. Draw the shapes of the parts in pencil before you cut them, and measure each piece carefully.

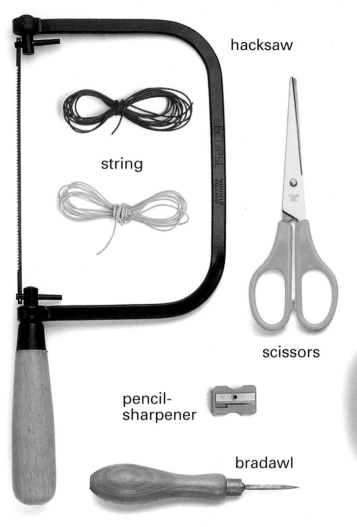

hacksaw

string

scissors

pencil-
sharpener

bradawl

Joining

A strong glue is the simplest way to join pieces of wood, cardboard, metal or plastic. It's easiest to use glue sticks and a glue gun, but many other glues work just as well. Before you use a glue always check that it is designed for the materials you are joining together. Screws, pins, adhesive tape and string can also be useful. Be sure to use waterproof glue and tape for the models in this book.

hairdrier

hand drill
and bits

Cutting

Cutting can be very dangerous, so always ask an adult to help you. A mortise saw is good for making straight cuts. For more complicated shapes, use a hacksaw or a craft knife. Smooth the pieces you cut with a file or sandpaper.

Drilling

Before you drill a hole in wood, mark the place in pencil. Start the hole with a bradawl, then finish it off with a hand drill.

Finishing and decorating

Balsa wood soaks up water, so paint your models with waterproof paints before putting them into water. Use glossy, acrylic or enamel paint. Waterproof tape is good for decorating models as well as for joining parts together.

Science and shipbuilding

When shipbuilders build boats they have to be both scientists and engineers. They must understand how the shape of a **hull** will affect its behavior in water and how the boat will handle in rough seas. They also need to know the best materials for the different parts of the ship and how powerful a ship's **engine** needs to be. Science and engineering can help shipbuilders to find out all these things.

Some things float, others sink—it seems simple, doesn't it? But if you look carefully at which materials float and which ones do not, you will find that it isn't so straightforward. Surprisingly, materials that sink in some situations, can be made to float in others.

You will need
paper clips
a block of wood
a ball of plasticine
a bowl or tank of water
a piece of expanded polystyrene
a block of ice (you can make this in the freezer)

1 Put the polystyrene, wood, ice and plasticine into the tank of water. When they have settled, watch how each one acts in the water.

MAKE it WORK!
The reason some materials float and others do not is because of their **density**. The density of a material is determined by its weight. For example, if you had a jar and filled it to the brim with water and weighed it, and then filled the same jar to the brim with gold, you would find that the gold weighed almost 20 times more than the water. This means that gold is almost 20 times denser than water. Materials that are less dense than water float.

2 You will see that the polystyrene hardly disturbs the water surface. This is because it is much less dense than water. Wood may feel heavy, but it is also less dense than water and floats. When water is frozen it becomes less dense, so a block of ice will float, even though most of it lies under the surface. Plasticine is more dense than water and sinks to the bottom. Find other suitable objects made of different materials and see if they float or sink in water.

Making things float

In the last experiment you saw a ball of plasticine sink to the bottom of the tank of water. But the plasticine can be made to float by changing its shape. Press the plasticine into a simple boat shape and put it back in the tank.

Now the plasticine floats. This is because the thinner, broader plasticine boat shape, together with the air inside it, is less dense than the water. Try making the plasticine into other boat shapes and see which floats best.

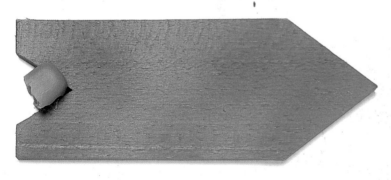

Surface tension

Although you cannot see it, the water surface acts like a thin elastic skin, and can support very light objects. This is called surface tension.

Paper clips are made of metal, but if you place them carefully on water they float. Dishwashing liquid breaks the water's surface tension. If you put a few drops of dishwashing liquid into the same water as the floating paper clips, the paper clips will sink.

Soap power

You can use surface tension to power a boat. Cut a simple boat shape out of balsa wood, as shown above. Then cut a V-shaped notch at the **stern** (the back) and wedge a piece of soap into it. Put the boat in the water and watch it go.

The boat works by reducing the surface tension of the water behind it. As the surface tension is broken by the soap, it pushes the boat away. For best results, use clean water.

8 Displacement

When you put an object in water, some of the water gets pushed aside to make room for it. This is called displacement of water. The water that has been displaced tries to reach the level of the rest of the water, and so pushes against the object. The more water an object displaces, the harder the water pushes.

MAKE it WORK!

This experiment shows how the weight of the water displaced by an object is the same as the weight of the object itself.

3 Note down the weight of the water.

4 Gently lower the plasticine boat into the water. Some of the water will spill out into the tray, but if you check the scales you will find that the reading stays the same.

5 Remove the boat from the water and lift the pan off the scales, taking care not to let any more water spill into the tray. Tip the water out. Take the scales out of the tray and replace the empty pan. Pour the water that spilled into the tray at step 4 into the scales.

6 Check the weight of the water. You will find that it is the same as the weight of the plasticine boat.

1 Weigh the plasticine.　　**2** Fill the pan.　　**3** Weigh the water.

You will need

a jug　　　　　　　　a pencil and paper
plasticine
a deep tray or a plastic bowl
scales with a deep weighing pan

1 Make the plasticine into the shape of a simple boat. Place it on the scales and note down the weight.

2 Put the scales in the tray and fill the weighing pan with water right up to the brim. Don't let any water spill into the tray.

Your displacement power

Next time you get into the bathtub, note the level of the water and watch the level rise as you get in. If you relax your arms and legs you will feel the water pushing them to the surface, but it is unlikely that the bathtub will hold enough water to support your full weight and make you float.

The more water an object displaces, the harder the water around it pushes back. This is why enormous modern supertankers can carry up to 300,000 tons of oil and still float.

fresh water   salt water

A hydrometer

Water has different densities. Warm water is not as dense as hot water, and fresh water is not as dense as salt water. In each type of water, a ship floats at a slightly different level. The density of water can be measured with a hydrometer.

◀ You can make a simple hydrometer by putting a small ball of plasticine on the end of a straw. Put the hydrometer in a glass of water at room temperature and mark where it meets the surface of the water. Then make up a mixture of salt and water and replace the hydrometer. The straw will float higher because the salt water is more dense.

4 Add the boat.   **5** Pour the spilled water back.   **6** Weigh the water.

The Plimsoll line

The Plimsoll line is a series of lines on the side of a ship to show the limit of the load it can carry in different waters, each with a different density. In this picture, the marks on the left show the level a ship should float in tropical fresh water (**TF**) and fresh water (**F**). The marks on the right show the levels in seawater in the tropics (**T**), in summer (**S**), in winter (**W**) and in winter in the North Atlantic (**WNA**). These lines are vital for safety because if a ship sails from one type of water to another, it might sink dangerously low in the water.

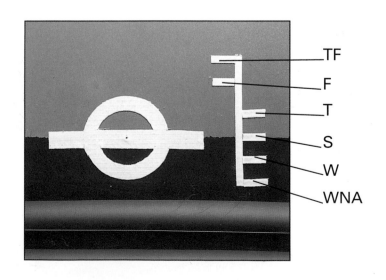

10 Wood and Skin Boats

People probably first traveled in water using logs or other light materials as floats. But they soon learned to make rafts by tying several logs together. Where wood was scarce, they made rafts of reeds or inflated animal skins.

MAKE it WORK!

Skin boats were a step up from rafts because they were watertight. This light fishing **coracle** had a flexible willow framework with an animal-skin covering.

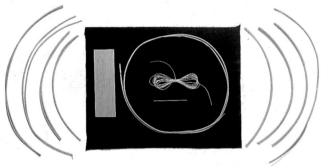

To make a coracle you will need

cotton cloth	waterproof glue
a darning needle	white glue
strong thread for sewing	varnish
a small piece of balsa wood	string
a 10 ft. length of basket cane	
16 lengths of 12 in. basket cane	

1 Curve the long piece of basket cane to make a circle of double thickness. Tie the ends together with string. This will be the rim of the coracle.

2 Tie five pairs of short canes across this circle, evenly spaced like ribs. Weave the other three pairs of canes lengthwise across the first five, tying them where they cross.

3 Press in the sides of the frame to form an oval. For a seat, cut the balsa wood to fit the narrowest width of the boat. Use waterproof glue to fix in position as shown below left.

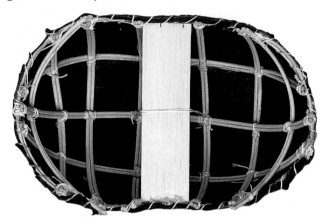

4 To cover the boat, stretch the cotton over the frame and secure it with one stitch in each corner. Trim the cotton to fit. Sew the cotton to the edge of the frame. Tie string to a cane on either side of the seat as shown above, to make a handle for carrying your coracle.

5 Paint the outside of the cloth with white glue and leave it to dry overnight. The white glue will make the cloth shrink, so that it fits really tightly over the frame.

6 Most white glues are not waterproof, so give your skin boat a coat of varnish to make it watertight. When completely dry, your coracle is ready to put on the water.

MAKE it WORK!
Another simple way to build a boat is to hollow out a log and make a dugout **canoe**. Dugouts are heavy and narrow, and so only good for river travel. But a dugout can be stabilized for sea travel by adding a float called an **outrigger**.

To make a dugout canoe you will need
balsa wood	glue
a craft knife	paint
three wooden skewers	sandpaper

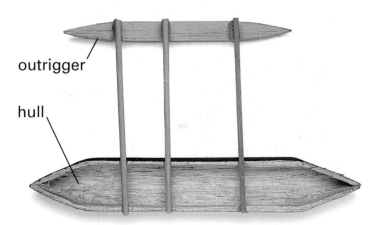

outrigger

hull

1 Cut the balsa-wood hull and outrigger in the shapes shown above. Then ask an adult to help you roughly hollow out the hull with a craft knife. Smooth both pieces with sandpaper.

2 Glue the wooden skewers across the dugout hull as shown. Cut balsa-wood spacers to go between the skewers and the outrigger. These are to ensure that when the boat sits on the water, the hull and the outrigger are level, so you will need to judge their size carefully.

3 Glue the spacers to the wooden skewers, then glue the outrigger to the spacers. Now paint your dugout and it is ready for its first trip.

Paddles
The coracle and the dugout on these pages would probably have been controlled using a paddle. It would have been a short paddle, so that it could be dipped into the water either side of the boat to push it along, steer it and act as a brake. Ask an adult to help you shape one out of balsa wood using a craft knife.

Many coracles were light and easy to carry. If there were dangerous rapids, or if strong currents made paddling upstream impossible, you slung the coracle onto your back and walked overland. But some coracles were heavier. Around 3,000 years ago in Assyria (part of modern Iraq), they were built to carry chariots or loads of building stone. A dugout canoe with an outrigger would be too heavy to carry very far, but lighter, portable canoes were built of skin for this purpose.

The earliest boats were simple shapes because building techniques were very basic. But as builders became more skilled they learned to shape a boat to suit its purpose. The part of the boat that has the most effect on how the boat moves is the section in contact with the water: the hull.

Experiment with hull shapes

There are two main hull shapes: broad hulls for carrying cargo, and long, thin hulls for traveling at speed. See for yourself how different shapes travel by making some simple hulls and pushing them around in a tank of water. How quickly do they move? How stable are they if you swirl the water about? How heavy a load can the different hull shapes carry?

▲ When this block of wood is put into the water (see below), it tips to one side. This is because the density of the wood is uneven, which makes the block very unstable. It would not be suitable for making a boat.

▼ Cut a long, thin shape from balsa wood like the one below and see how quickly it moves. **Energy** is wasted pushing a flat end, or nose, through the water, so most hulls are pointed to help them cut through the water.

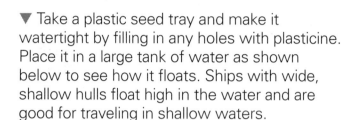

▼ Take a plastic seed tray and make it watertight by filling in any holes with plasticine. Place it in a large tank of water as shown below to see how it floats. Ships with wide, shallow hulls float high in the water and are good for traveling in shallow waters.

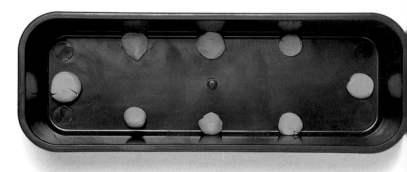

What is a keel?

The **keel** of a boat is the part of the hull that sits underwater. It keeps the boat stable and stops it from being blown sideways or overturned by the wind. Keels come in many shapes. A broad, deep keel is very stable but it makes the boat slow. Racing boats use a slim, narrow keel.

MAKE it WORK!

The first **yachts** had large, heavy keels running the length of the boat. But modern yachts have deep, narrow keels right in the center. Make boats with the two different types of keel and compare how they move through the water.

For a large-keeled hull you will need

glue, paint and plasticine   balsa wood
a hand drill   a craft knife

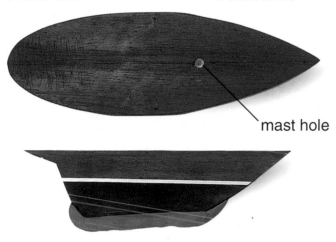

mast hole

1 Cut out a balsa-wood hull 3 x 8 in., and a keel 9 in. long x 2¹/₂ in. deep. Drill a mast hole as shown. Paint the pieces and leave them to dry. Fix some plasticine along the keel.

keel

2 Glue the pieces together and float the large-keeled hull in water. The plasticine will add weight to the keel and keep the hull upright. Turn to page 18 to find out how to make sails.

For a narrow-keeled hull you will need

balsa wood   a hacksaw
tape, glue and paint   a hand drill
pliers and thick wire   a sheet of brass

1 Cut the hull and cabin shapes from balsa wood. Drill a small hole at the back of the boat for the **rudder** and one at the front for the mast. Paint all these parts and leave to dry.

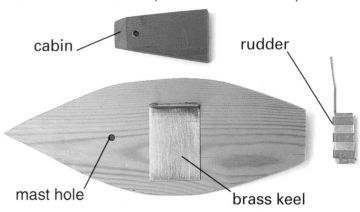

cabin   rudder

mast hole   brass keel

2 Glue the cabin to the hull. Using the hacksaw, cut a brass strip for the rudder. Bend the wire into a long L-shape as wide as the rudder. Tape the rudder into the corner of the L. Push the other wire end through the hole at the stern. Bend it over to hold in place and make a **tiller**.

tiller

3 Cut the brass keel. Use pliers to bend over one short edge at a right angle and glue the flap to the bottom of the hull. Because the brass is heavy, the hull will stay upright in the water.

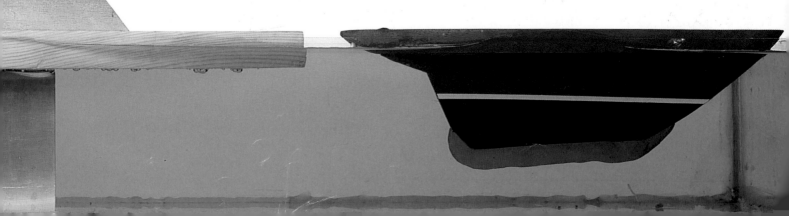

Boats were probably first moved along by paddling with the hands. But it did not take long before people invented paddles, which are bigger and can push more water. Oars are more efficient than paddles because they use the natural spring of the wood. Also, the rowing action uses more of the body's muscles, to give a stronger pull.

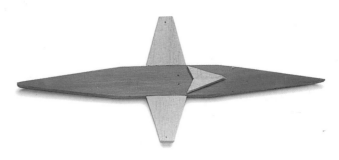

1 Cut out the hull 16 x 1½ in., outriggers 2⅓ x 2 in., and spray deck 2⅓ in. long. Paint, and when dry make a hole in the tip of each outrigger as shown above. Glue them to either side of the hull and then glue the spray deck in front of the outriggers.

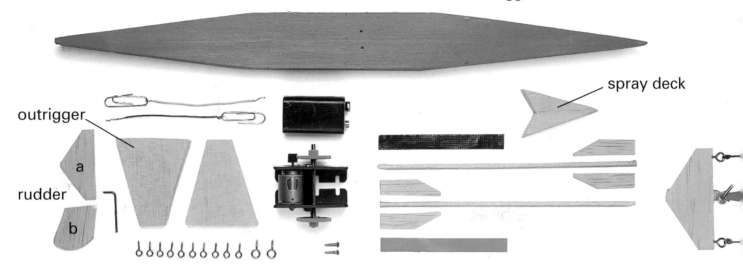

spray deck

outrigger

a

rudder

b

MAKE it WORK!

This rowing model is based on a racing boat called a **single scull**. It uses a battery instead of muscle power, but it copies the action of a real rower quite closely.

You will need

paper clips	stiff wire
small screws	brass eyelets
glue and tape	electrical wire
a 9-volt flat battery	thin string or thread

an electric motor and gearbox
1 in. thick balsa wood for the hull
⅕ in. thick balsa wood for spray deck and outriggers
1/10 in. thick balsa wood for the rudder and oar blades
thin dowel to fit in the holes in the gearbox and through brass eyelets

2 Cut out the two rudder shapes marked **a** 2 x 1 in. and **b** 1 x 1½ in. Paint, and when dry glue piece **b** across the center of piece **a**. Screw four eyelets into the rudder and two into the back of the hull, as shown above. Bend the top of a piece of stiff wire. Position the rudder so that the eyelets on its back line up with those on the hull, then thread the wire through to hold the two together.

yoke

3 Screw six eyelets to the hull and outriggers as shown above. Thread the string (shown above in red and green) in a loop from one of the eyelets in the yoke at the top of the rudder, through the four eyelets on the hull, back to the second eyelet on the rudder.

5 Screw the motor and tape the battery to the hull. Position them carefully to balance the boat before you fix them—the hull should not lean to one side, and the **bows** should not lift out of the water or sink below the surface.

6 Cut the four oar blades, 2 in. long. Paint, and when dry glue them to the ends of two pieces of thin dowel 7 in. long. Add some tape round the blades for strength. Thread the oars through the eyelets on the outriggers.

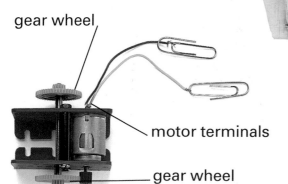

7 Put glue on the end of each oar. Push each oar into one of the holes round the outside of the gear wheels. Connect the paper clips to the battery terminals and the oars will start to turn.

gear wheel

motor terminals

gear wheel

4 Put together the motor and gearbox as shown above. Then attach the electric wires to the terminals on the motor at one end, and to the paper clips at the other end.

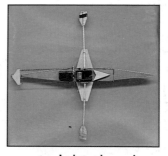

straight ahead

turning left

Using the rudder

A rudder is a vertical panel that sits in the water at the back of the boat. It allows you to control the direction you travel in. Experiment to find out which way the boat heads when you turn the rudder to the left and the right.

Pictures from over 5,000 years ago show Egyptian boats with a single square sail. These early sailing boats could only follow the direction of the wind. About 1,000 years ago, Viking ships were still using a square sail, but relied on oar power to change their course.

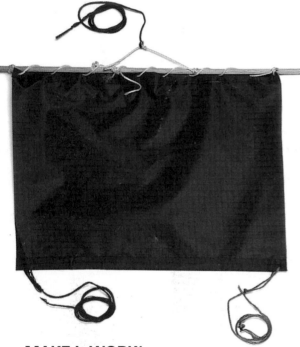

MAKE it WORK!
The Vikings used a square sail and oars for their cargo carriers and speedy longships. This Viking ship uses ropes to turn the sail, so the ship can take better advantage of the wind.

You will need
a hand drill	string, glue and paint
balsa wood	a darning needle
brass eyelets	strong thread
$1/10$ in. and $1/5$ in. dowel	
ripstop nylon or other light, strong cloth	

1 Cut a hull shape 10 x $2^4/_5$ in., and a mast block 3 x $1/2$ in. out of balsa wood. Paint the hull. Drill a $1/3$ in. hole in the mast block and then glue it in the center of the hull. Screw six eyelets into the hull as marked above right.

2 Cut two lengths of dowel: $1/5$ x 8 in. for the mast and $1/10$ x 7 in. for the **spar**. Screw in one eyelet at the top of the mast and one near the bottom. Drill a small hole $1/3$ in. from the top of the mast. Glue the mast into the hole in the mast block.

3 Cut out a sail $6^1/2$ x 6 in. Fold over and glue the bottom and top edges for strength. Use a needle to thread two lengths of string (the **main sheets**) through the bottom corners of the sail. Knot to secure them to the sail.

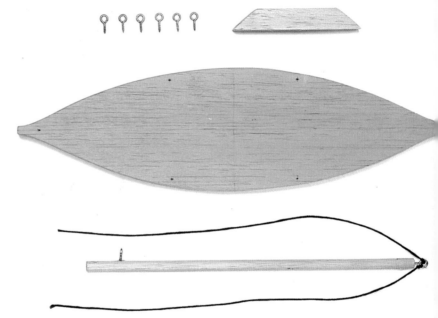

4 To make the **halyard** (the rope for raising and lowering the sail), tie a piece of string firmly to either side of the center of the spar. Tie the uphaul thread to this short string as shown in the picture below. Using the darning needle, sew the sail to the spar as below.

tying the halyard   sewing the sail

5 Support the mast with two stays (ropes running **fore and aft** from the mast). Put the sail in position against the mast and pull the halyard thread through the hole near the top of the mast. Pull the spar up as far as it will go, then tie the halyard thread to the eyelet at the bottom of the mast. Tie the main sheets to the eyelets on the hull as shown below.

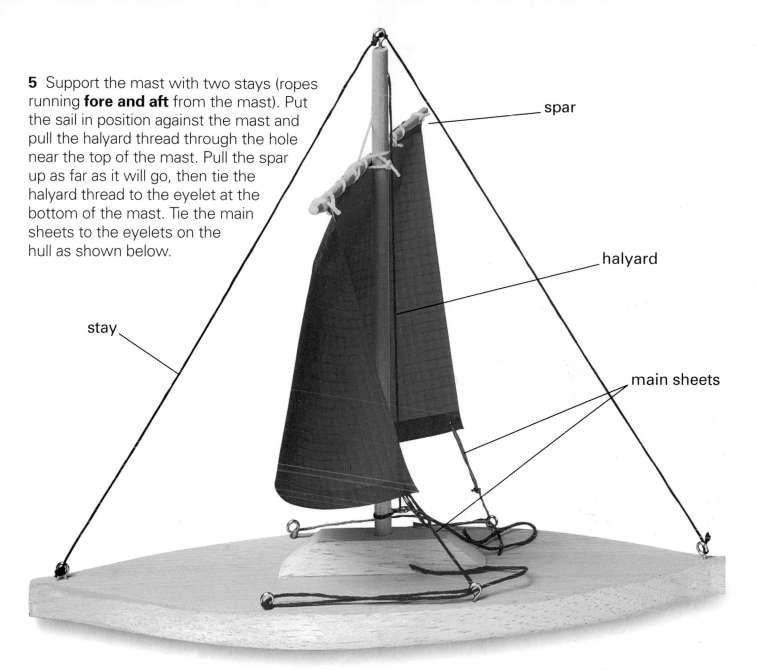

spar

halyard

stay

main sheets

6 Your Viking ship is now ready to sail. Like a real Viking ship it doesn't have a back or a front. To sail in the opposite direction you just move the sail to the other side of the mast.

7 By adjusting the main sheets you can slightly turn the sails from side to side, but you will find that this is limited compared to modern ships.

▼ There are two sets of eyelets on the deck, so the sail can be set on either side of the mast.

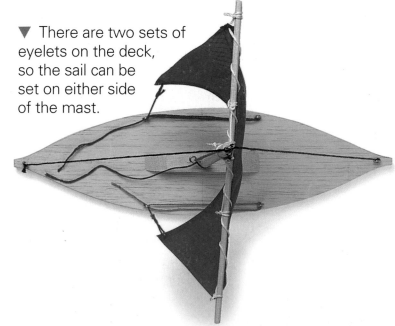

The first sail may well have been a giant palm leaf. Boats with palm-leaf sails were built in West Africa until the 19th century.

The **rig** is the arrangement of sails on a ship. The simplest rig is one square sail, but two sails set in line with the hull, running from front to back, are more efficient. This is a fore–and–aft rig.

MAKE it WORK!

Make these two ships with different fore-and-aft rigs and compare how they handle. The **dhow** has a **lateen** made up of one or two masts with large triangular sails. The **cutter** has only one mast, but its rig, with the extra spar, or **gaff**, is more flexible.

To make a dhow you will need

a darning needle	a hand drill
balsa wood blocks	ripstop nylon
string, glue and paint	brass eyelets
$1/10$ in. and $1/5$ in. dowel	

1 Cut a balsa-wood hull 3 x 8 in., and a keel 9 x $2^1/_2$ in. Paint and glue together.

2 From $1/5$ in. dowel cut two masts: one 7 in. long, the other $5^1/_2$ in. Drill a small hole near the top of each. From $1/10$ in. dowel cut two spars: one 11 in. long, the other 8 in.

3 From $1/10$ in. dowel cut a 6 in. **bowsprit**. Screw 12 eyelets to the hull as shown above right, and one to the end of the bowsprit.

4 Drill two holes for masts in the hull and glue the masts in position. Secure with three strings tied to the eyelets on the hull. Slide the bowsprit through two eyelets and glue it to the mast.

5 Now cut out the sails to fit the spars, as shown below left. Allow $1/5$ in. overlap on the long edge of each sail. Fold and glue the long edge of each sail over its spar. Thread strings through the bottom corners of both sails. Thread and tie a string around each spar, two-thirds of the way up.

bowsprit

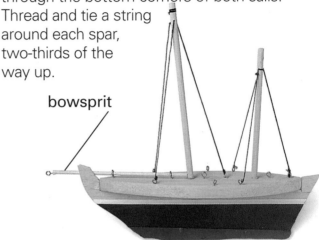

6 Thread the string for each spar through the eyelet hole at the top of the mast. Pull the sails up as high as they will go and tie each string to the eyelet at the base of the mast. Attach the strings from the bottom corners of the sails to the eyelets on the hull as shown.

lateen rig

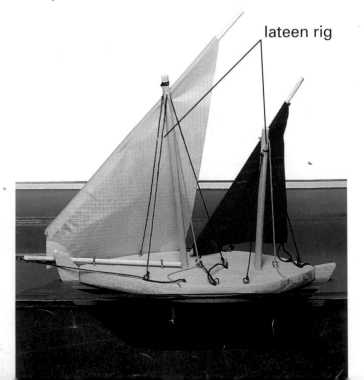

To make a cutter you will need

brass eyelets
ripstop nylon
balsa wood blocks
$^1/_{10}$ in. and $^1/_5$ in. dowel
the large-keeled hull from pages 12 and 13

string and glue
a screw-in hook
a darning needle

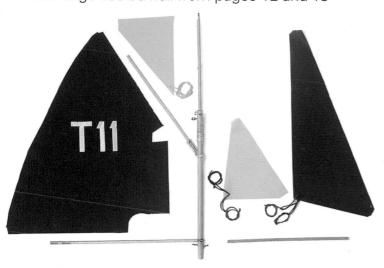

1 From $^1/_5$ in. dowel cut a mast 7 in. long. From $^1/_{10}$ in. dowel cut a boom 8 in. long, a gaff $6^1/_4$ in. long, a bowsprit 6 in. long and a topmast $6^1/_5$ in. long. Drill a hole in the hull for the mast.

2 Screw an eyelet into the top of the topmast. Glue and tie the topmast to the mast. Fasten the boom to the mast with a hook and eyelet.

3 Push the complete mast into the hole in the hull and secure with glue. Loop some string around the mast and then around one end of the gaff as shown above. Screw two eyelets to the hull, slide the bowsprit through and glue to the mast, as above.

4 Cut out four sails as shown left, allowing a $^1/_5$ in. edge for gluing. Thread the strings through the bottom corners. Attach all the strings as shown in the picture right.

5 Glue the short edge of the topsail over the string, between the gaff and the topmast.

6 Screw an eyelet to the top of the mast. Run the string at the bottom of the topsail through it.

7 Glue the edges of the **mainsail** around the mast, gaff and boom. Glue the long edges of the foresails over the strings between the bowsprit and the mast. Tie the corners to eyelets on the hull as shown below. Now your cutter is ready to set sail.

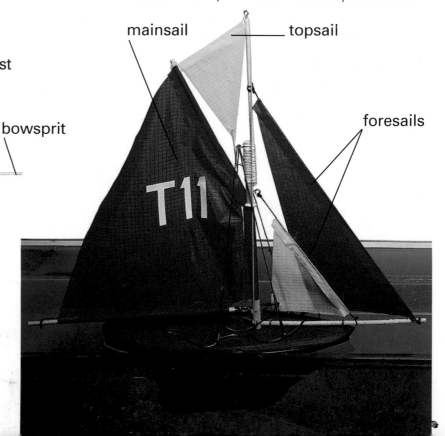

20 Modern Sailing Boats

The arrangement of the sails on most modern yachts is called a **Bermuda rig**, also known as a sloop. It is very efficient. The triangular sails give the most pull and the least drag, and two of them can harness more wind power than one. The fastest ships have tiny hulls, with tall sails to pull them along.

MAKE it WORK!

This modern Bermuda-rigged sailing dinghy has a **centerboard**, or adjustable keel, to make it sail safely and more efficiently.

You will need

ripstop nylon or any other strong, light cloth
$1/10$ in. and $1/5$ in. dowel
a small screw-in hook
a mapping pin
brass eyelets   glue and paint
balsa wood   a craft knife
                       string

1 Cut a balsa-wood hull shape, 8 x 3 in. Paint and leave to dry. Make six small holes and screw in six eyelets. With an adult's help, cut a slit for the centerboard with a craft knife.

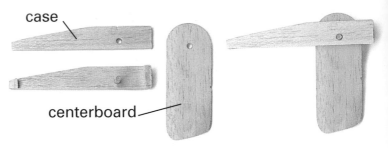

case

centerboard

2 Cut the case pieces and the centerboard from balsa wood. Paint the centerboard and leave it to dry. Drill a hole about $1/10$ in. thick in each piece, ensuring that all three holes line up. Cut two balsa-wood blocks and glue one to each end of one of the case pieces as shown above.

3 Place glue on each block and stick the two case pieces together. Cut a small piece of dowel and slide it through the holes in the centerboard and case. Make sure that the centerboard remains free to move inside the slit on the hull. Now slot the centerboard into the slit on the hull. Glue the case to the hull.

4 Cut two $1/5$ in. dowels, $9 1/2$ in. and 4 in. long, for the mast and the boom. Screw two eyelets into the mast and a hook into the boom as shown below. Hook the boom to the mast and glue the mast to the hull.

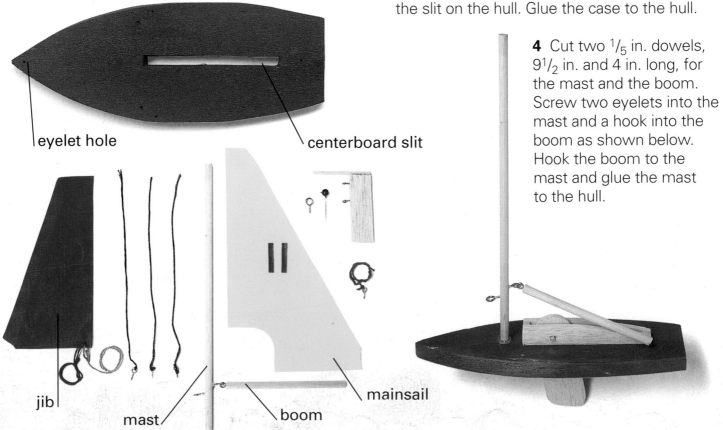

eyelet hole

centerboard slit

jib

mast

boom

mainsail

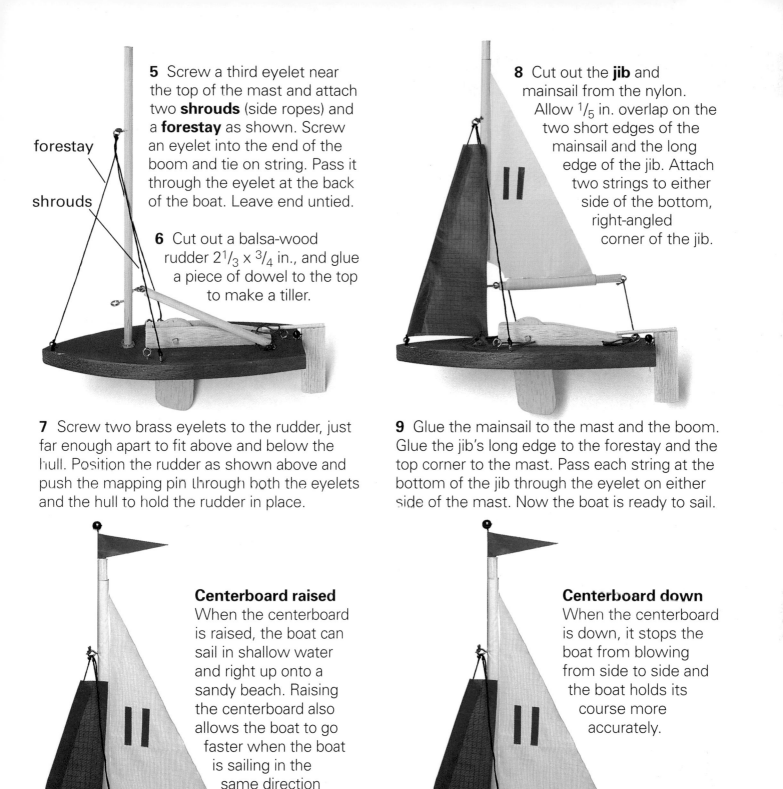

5 Screw a third eyelet near the top of the mast and attach two **shrouds** (side ropes) and a **forestay** as shown. Screw an eyelet into the end of the boom and tie on string. Pass it through the eyelet at the back of the boat. Leave end untied.

forestay

shrouds

6 Cut out a balsa-wood rudder $2^{1}/_{3} \times {}^{3}/_{4}$ in., and glue a piece of dowel to the top to make a tiller.

8 Cut out the **jib** and mainsail from the nylon. Allow $^{1}/_{5}$ in. overlap on the two short edges of the mainsail and the long edge of the jib. Attach two strings to either side of the bottom, right-angled corner of the jib.

7 Screw two brass eyelets to the rudder, just far enough apart to fit above and below the hull. Position the rudder as shown above and push the mapping pin through both the eyelets and the hull to hold the rudder in place.

9 Glue the mainsail to the mast and the boom. Glue the jib's long edge to the forestay and the top corner to the mast. Pass each string at the bottom of the jib through the eyelet on either side of the mast. Now the boat is ready to sail.

Centerboard raised
When the centerboard is raised, the boat can sail in shallow water and right up onto a sandy beach. Raising the centerboard also allows the boat to go faster when the boat is sailing in the same direction as the wind.

Centerboard down
When the centerboard is down, it stops the boat from blowing from side to side and the boat holds its course more accurately.

A boat would not be much use if it could only sail with the wind behind it. Luckily, sails are very versatile and can use the wind to get you wherever you want to go. However, you may not be able to travel directly. If you need to travel into the oncoming wind you have to take a zigzag course. This is called **tacking**.

7 Sailing with the wind directly behind you is known as "running before the wind." To use the sails efficiently they should be "goose-winged," which means that the mainsail is right out to one side of the boat, while the jib is right out to the other.

Controlling a yacht

To sail a boat efficiently you have to learn to control many different parts of the vessel at the same time. Following the course of this small yacht around the page will help you to begin to understand how the different parts work together to use the power of the wind.

1 When a boat is sailing as nearly into the wind as it can, it is said to be "close-hauled." This means that the sails are pulled in as close to the hull as possible. In this position, while part of the force of the wind tries to push the boat sideways, the rest of it pushes the boat forward.

2 Each stage of the zigzag is called a tack. To change tack the crew needs to control the boat so that the wind catches the other side of the sail. To prepare for this, the boat must gradually steer farther and farther into the wind.

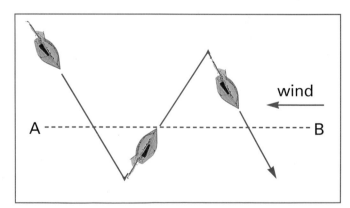

A .... B

wind →

▲ The boat in this picture wants to sail from A to B, but because of the direction of the wind it must tack there. On these pages, the wind is blowing from right to left and the boat makes just one tack in a similar zigzag course, as shown above, before turning round.

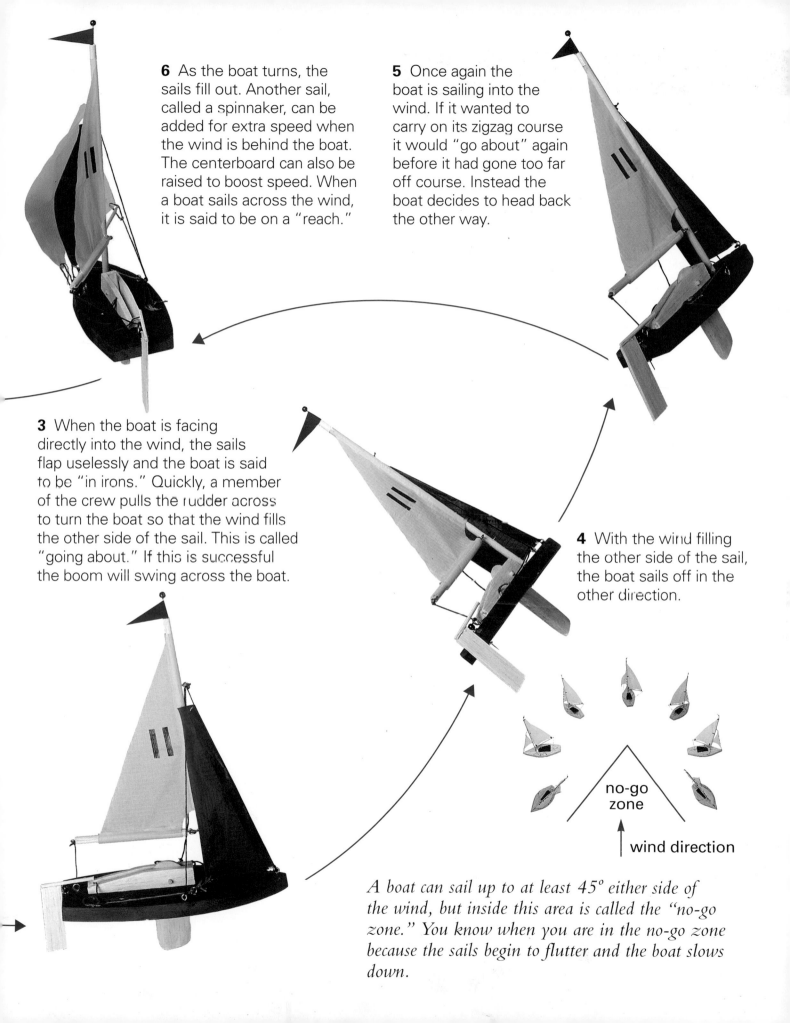

6 As the boat turns, the sails fill out. Another sail, called a spinnaker, can be added for extra speed when the wind is behind the boat. The centerboard can also be raised to boost speed. When a boat sails across the wind, it is said to be on a "reach."

5 Once again the boat is sailing into the wind. If it wanted to carry on its zigzag course it would "go about" again before it had gone too far off course. Instead the boat decides to head back the other way.

3 When the boat is facing directly into the wind, the sails flap uselessly and the boat is said to be "in irons." Quickly, a member of the crew pulls the rudder across to turn the boat so that the wind fills the other side of the sail. This is called "going about." If this is successful the boom will swing across the boat.

4 With the wind filling the other side of the sail, the boat sails off in the other direction.

no-go zone

↑ wind direction

A boat can sail up to at least 45° either side of the wind, but inside this area is called the "no-go zone." You know when you are in the no-go zone because the sails begin to flutter and the boat slows down.

24 Steamships

In the 18th century, a new way to power boats was discovered— the steam engine. The steam engine works because when water is boiled it turns to steam, which takes up much more space than water. The force of the expanding steam is channeled into turning a wheel that propels the boat.

Until the invention of the steam engine, boats had been powered only by wind or human muscles!

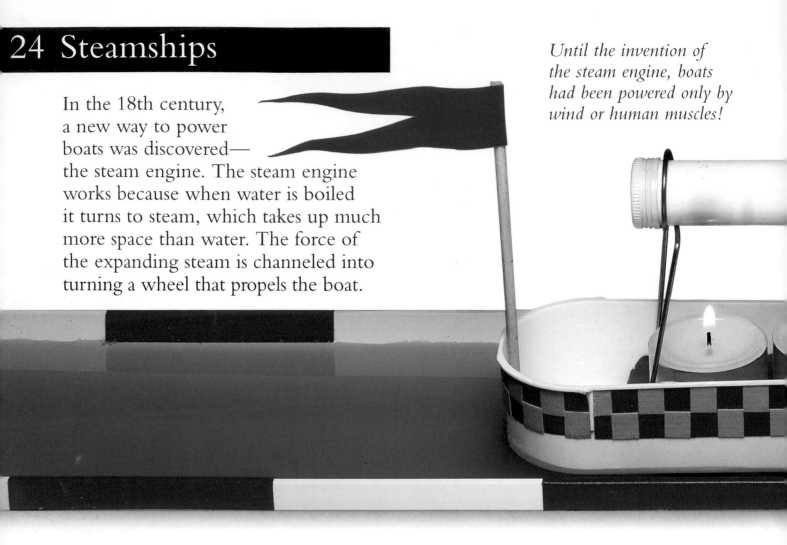

MAKE it WORK!

Unlike standard steamships, this candle-powered boat doesn't use steam power to turn a wheel. Instead, the steam shoots out of the back in a high-pressure jet that pushes the boat along.

You will need

a thin dowel
three votive candles
two pieces of stiff wire
a plastic box about 8 x 3 in.
colored tape and cardboard
a dowel slightly thicker than the cigar tube

glue
a bradawl
plasticine
a cigar tube

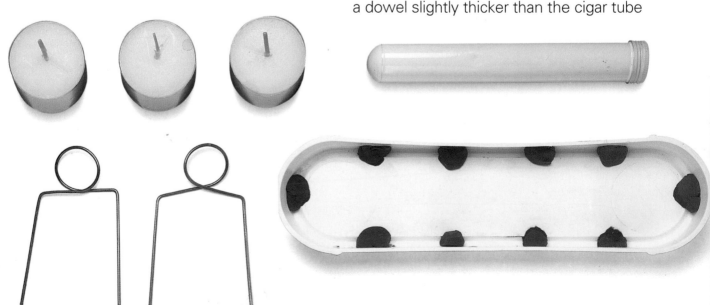

1 Fill any holes in the box with plasticine. If you are going to decorate the box with colored tape and a flag you should do it at this point. Glue the candles firmly into the bottom of the boat as shown below.

4 Place the boat in water and light the candles. The water in the cigar tube will quickly boil and steam will begin to escape out of the back. As the steam pushes its way through the tiny hole the boat will move forward.

Be very careful!
Handle your boat with an adult's help, as the cigar tube can get very hot. The steam can also be hot, so keep your hands and face well away from the back of the boat when it is moving along. Never leave lit candles unattended.

Speed control
Try some experiments with your steamboat. If you add a little more water it will take longer to heat up, but the boat will travel farther. If you shorten the wires so that the candles are a little closer to the tube, it will heat up the water more quickly and travel faster. But don't make the hole at the back of the cigar tube too big. If you make it too easy for the steam to escape it will not push the boat forward.

2 Make the supports for the cigar tube by bending the wire around a piece of thick dowel, as shown above.

3 Using the bradawl, make a small hole in the cigar-tube cap. Then slide the wire loops over the end of the cigar tube and tighten them until they hold the tube firmly. Fill the tube about one-third with water, screw on the cap and fix the whole assembly into the boat with plasticine.

The first steamboats began carrying passengers along the rivers of the United States and Britain from about 1810. By the 1840s there were regular steamship services across the Atlantic Ocean. Throughout the late 19th and early 20th centuries, liners became even faster and more luxurious, as rival steamship companies competed for passengers.

26 Paddle Steamers

The first steamboats used large paddle-wheels to move them through the water. The paddles acted like a set of rotating oars. There were two types of paddle steamer: stern-wheelers, which had a large paddle-wheel at the stern, and side-wheelers which used two smaller paddle-wheels, one on each side.

MAKE it WORK!

Side-wheelers were steered by their paddle-wheels and the rudder, but this electric model can be steered only by the paddle-wheels.

You will need

glue	a cork
plasticine	paint
a bradawl	
balsa wood	
two cotton reels	
a plastic seed tray	
wire and paper clips	
a piece of thin dowel	
two 9-volt flat batteries	
four screws and washers	
two lengths of $1/5$ in. dowel	
two electric motors (with brackets)	

1 Make the seed tray watertight by filling any holes with plasticine. Add a ball of plasticine at each end so that it supports the deck and acts as **ballast**. For the deck, cut a piece of balsa wood to fit in the tray. Cut out three rectangles from the balsa wood deck as shown below left.

2 Cut 12 pieces of balsa wood, $4/5$ x 1 in., for the paddles. Paint, and when dry glue six paddles around the edge of each cotton reel as shown above. Cut two sections of cork about $2/5$ in. thick, and glue one to the end of each cotton reel. Using the bradawl, make a small hole in the center of the cork.

bowsprit

3 Measure the width of the seed tray and cut a strip of balsa wood that will just fit inside it. Paint and leave to dry. Screw an electric motor on each end. Fill the hole in the cork on each paddle with glue. Now glue a paddle-wheel onto the spindle of each electric motor.

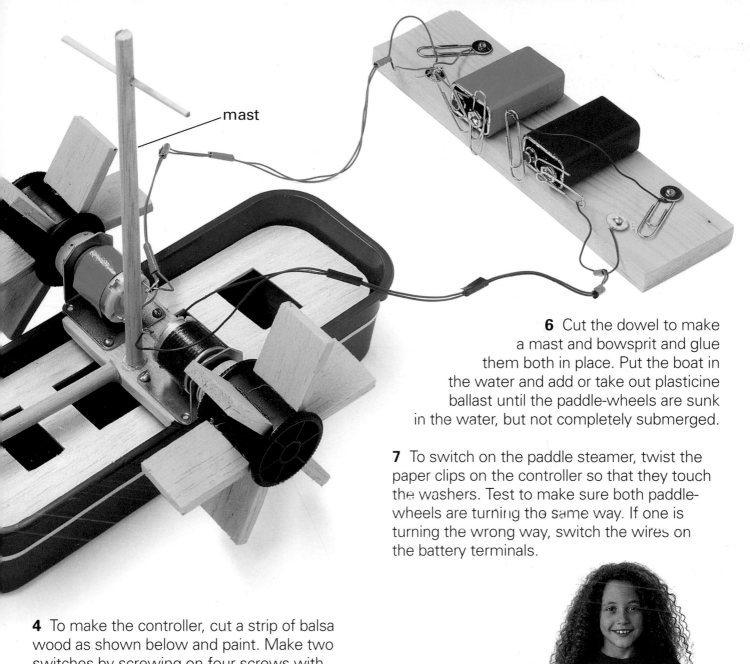

mast

6 Cut the dowel to make a mast and bowsprit and glue them both in place. Put the boat in the water and add or take out plasticine ballast until the paddle-wheels are sunk in the water, but not completely submerged.

7 To switch on the paddle steamer, twist the paper clips on the controller so that they touch the washers. Test to make sure both paddle-wheels are turning the same way. If one is turning the wrong way, switch the wires on the battery terminals.

4 To make the controller, cut a strip of balsa wood as shown below and paint. Make two switches by screwing on four screws with washers. Put a paper clip under two of the washers. Glue the batteries to the balsa wood.

5 Using the picture above to help you, connect one terminal of each battery to the terminal of one of the motors. Connect the other battery terminal to the paper clip side of the switch. The negative terminal of the motor connects to the washer part of the switch.

Different maneuvers
First, try out the boat with both motors on, then turn one off and see what happens. You could also put the paddle-wheels into reverse by switching the wires on each battery.

28 Motorboats

When a motor turns a propeller in the water it pushes water backwards away from the boat, which moves the boat forward. The more water a propeller pushes away, the faster the boat will go. To make a fast boat you need to find the balance between a large propeller and a powerful engine to turn it. If the engine is too large it will also be heavy and slow down the boat.

MAKE it WORK!

When measuring the pieces for this **catamaran** motorboat, judge the size of the hulls by the length of your propeller shaft. The motor must sit in the middle of the boat and the propeller must be well under the water.

You will need

Velcro
stiff wire
paper clips
a hand drill
U-shaped pin
electrical wire
strips of brass
a propeller shaft
a 9-volt flat battery
glue, tape and paint
an electric motor and bracket
sheets of balsa wood   pliers
two sizes of propeller   a rubber grommet
balsa wood or polystyrene for the hull
copper tubing that fits over the propeller shaft

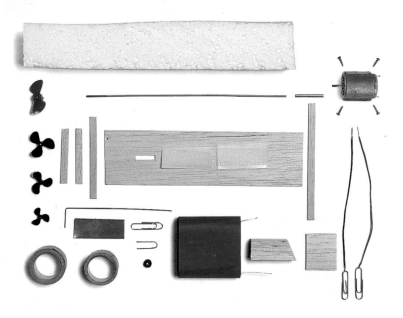

rudder

1 Shape two hulls 8 x 1 in. and 1¹/₂ in. deep from balsa or polystyrene. Cut a deck 6 x 2¹/₃ in. and make a ³/₄ in. slit in it. Paint the hulls and the deck. Glue a strip of balsa wood to the back edge and drill two holes as shown. Glue Velcro to the deck and glue the deck to the hulls.

4 Push the propeller shaft through the slit in the deck to almost meet the motor spindle. Slide the grommet onto the shaft. Slide a piece of copper tube over the end of the propeller shaft and motor spindle and crimp the tube with pliers to grip them both.

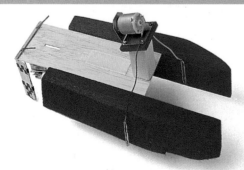

2 Make a stand from two pieces of balsa, as above, and screw the motor and bracket to it. Glue the stand to the deck. Attach wires with paper clips on the end to the motor terminals.

3 For the rudders, tape two brass rectangles to two pieces of wire as shown at left. Thread the wires through the holes in the deck.

5 Hold the rubber grommet in place by fixing it to the deck with a U-shaped pin.

6 Glue a piece of Velcro to the battery, and fix the battery to the deck as shown. Position the battery so that its weight slightly raises the bow (the front) of the boat. Then connect the motor and the battery with the paper clips and your motorboat will speed away.

7 Try the boat with a small propeller, then with a larger one. With a large propeller the boat should go faster, but if the motor is not very powerful it may not be able to turn the large propeller fast enough.

A swamp skimmer travels over water powered by an air propeller. Because air is much lighter than water it gives less **thrust**, so the propeller must be much bigger than a water propeller.

MAKE it WORK!

This skimmer is perfect for swamps where an underwater propeller would clog up with weeds.

You will need

an electric motor and bracket
strong thread or string
sheet of balsa wood
electrical wire
balsa wood
a hand drill
a propeller
a 9-volt flat
 battery

paint
thin dowel
paper clips
brass eyelets
tape and glue

1 Shape two balsa hulls $8^1/_5$ x 1 in. and $1^1/_2$ in. deep. Cut two strips of balsa $5^1/_{10}$ in. long. Paint, and when dry glue together as shown.

2 Cut the upper deck $4^1/_5$ x 3 in. Cut two balsa uprights $4^1/_5$ in. long, and three horizontal strips: two 2 in. long and one $2^1/_3$ in. Paint, and when dry glue as shown below left.

3 Drill six holes in the hull. Glue four dowels at an angle into four holes as shown below left.

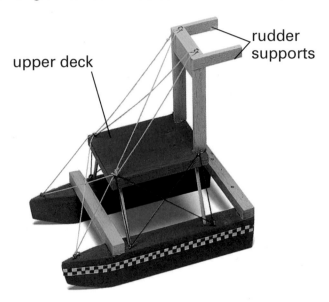

upper deck

rudder supports

4 Drill six holes in the upper deck: four under the deck and two in the rudder supports. Make two more holes in the balsa strip, directly beneath the rudder supports. Glue the dowels of the hull into the deck holes.

5 Screw 12 brass eyelets into your skimmer, and join them with thread, as shown above.

6 Attach the propeller to the motor spindle and screw the motor to the deck. Add wires with paper clips on the ends to the motor terminals.

7 Glue the battery to the upper deck, just in front of the motor.

8 For the rudders, cut two thin dowels to fit exactly in the sets of holes at the back of the boat. Insert the dowels, making sure that they can turn freely in their sockets.

Turning the air
These rudders work by turning the stream of air coming from the propeller, rather than a stream of water, to one side or the other. How do you think these rudders compare with rudders in the water?

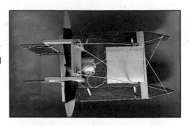

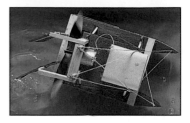

Swamp skimmers have shallow, flat-bottomed hulls so they can travel safely in water that is very shallow and often full of weeds or tree roots.

9 Cut the rudders from thin sheets of balsa wood. Paint and leave to dry. Glue and tape them into position as shown above.

10 Connect the paper clips to the battery terminals and the propeller will begin to turn. If the skimmer moves backward, switch the wires on the battery terminals.

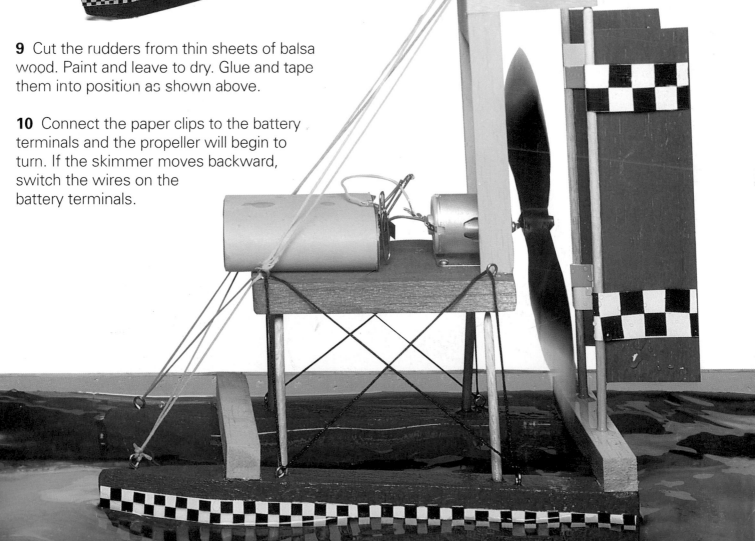

A hovercraft can travel over land or water because it floats just above the surface on its own cushion of air. Because a hovercraft does not have to push through water, it can travel much faster than a conventional ship. The cushion of air also gives a more comfortable ride because it does not have the rolling motion of a ship.

MAKE it WORK!

A hovercraft uses a powerful fan to draw in air from above the hovercraft. This air is then blown out below. A flexible rubber "skirt" around the hovercraft traps the air before it escapes. The model on this page does not have its own fan; instead the fan is in the hairdrier.

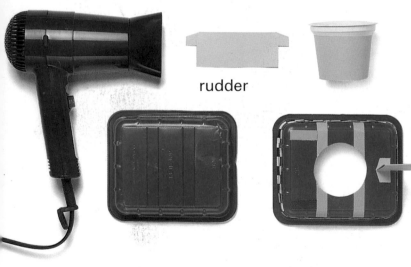

rudder

You will need

a craft knife
a plastic tray
tape and glue
a yogurt container with an opening larger than the hair-drier nozzle

a hairdrier
thin cardboard
a felt-tipped pen

1 Make sure that the tray is airtight by taping over any holes. Cut out the bottom of the yogurt container. Put the narrow end of the container on the center of the tray and draw round it.

2 Ask an adult to help you cut just outside the circle you have drawn using a craft knife. Glue the narrow end of the yogurt container firmly into the hole.

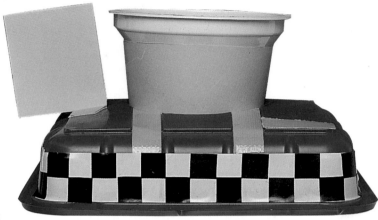

3 Cut the rudder shape out of thin cardboard, as shown below left, and fold it in half. Fold the two small tabs, one to each side, and glue them onto the hovercraft as shown above.

4 With the hairdrier on the coolest setting, point the nozzle at the mouth of the yogurt container and switch on. The hovercraft will rise into the air. By using the hairdrier at different angles you can make the hovercraft move forward or backward. If you bend the rudder slightly the model will turn too.

Be very careful!

Use this model only on a dry surface, **never** on water. Using electricity near water is extremely dangerous.

Hovercraft are called amphibious craft because they can travel over water and land. This means they are very versatile. Although they are used for crossing water, they actually begin their journeys on dry land. They just need a flat area of shore or tarmac, and are not affected by high and low tides or ice on the water. However hovercraft cannot be used in very rough weather conditions, because the cushion of air becomes unstable.

Test your steering skills

Make some course markers by sticking some paper flags onto toothpicks and pushing them into the bottom of some yogurt containers. Arrange the containers to make a zigzag course on the floor and test your skill at steering the hovercraft round it. Be careful not to pull on the cord of the hairdrier.

A submarine must be able to float on the water and to sink beneath it. To do this, it makes itself lighter or heavier using large tanks called ballast tanks along its sides. When the tanks are filled with air the submarine floats because air is light. To dive, the ballast tanks are filled with water. To get back to the surface, air is pumped back into the tanks to push out the water.

1 Take a rubber bottle stopper and draw round it twice on one side of the plastic bottle. Ask an adult to help you cut just outside the circles you have drawn using a craft knife. Fit the bottle stoppers tightly into the holes, as shown below. Now cut two slightly smaller holes in the opposite side of the submarine.

2 Make two small holes, one on each side of the bottle toward the back. Push a short length of the dowel through each hole. Cut two balsa-wood pieces (hydroplanes) in the shape shown below left, and paint them. Finally, glue the hydroplanes to the dowels.

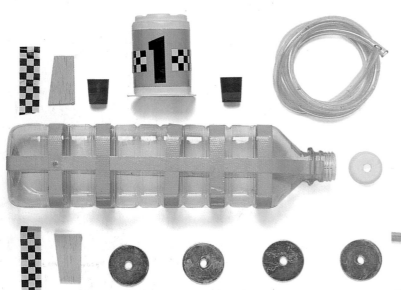

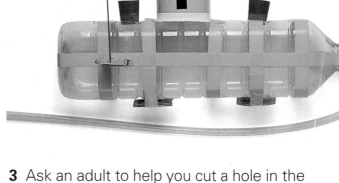

periscope

hydroplane

conning tower

MAKE it WORK!

This model submarine is made with a plastic bottle. Like a real submarine it dives and resurfaces by using water and air as ballast. As a submarine travels under the water, it needs a set of horizontal rudders, called hydroplanes, to control its movements up or down.

You will need

a craft knife	paint
balsa wood	plasticine
plastic tubing	thin dowel
large washers or coins	a hand drill
a plastic bottle with cap	waterproof tape
two rubber bottle stoppers	a yogurt container

3 Ask an adult to help you cut a hole in the bottle cap the same size as the plastic tubing. Push the tube into the cap, seal the edges with plasticine and screw the cap on tightly.

4 For the conning tower, decorate a yogurt container. Make a hole in the bottom and a small hole in the side so it can fill with water. Push a length of dowel through the hole to make a periscope, and glue the container to the submarine.

5 Tape the washers or coins to the bottom of the submarine at the front and back. You may need to experiment with two, three or four of these. They should provide enough weight to help the submarine sink when full of water, but not so much as to make it sink when full of air.

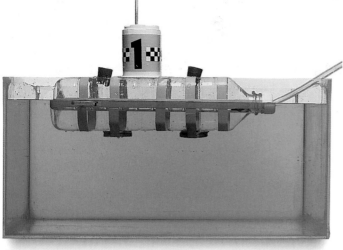

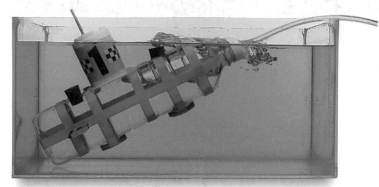

Operating your submarine

1 Put the submarine in water with the bottle stoppers in. When the submarine has taken in a little water and floats at the surface, stop the air from escaping by pinching the plastic tubing.

3 To make the submarine rise, put the stoppers back in while it is still underwater. Now blow hard into the plastic tubing. As the air pushes water out of the submarine it becomes lighter and rises to the top of the tank.

4 When you have blown out all the air, the submarine will sit on the surface of the water. As soon as you stop blowing, pinch the tubing to stop the air escaping or water will flood back in and the submarine will sink again.

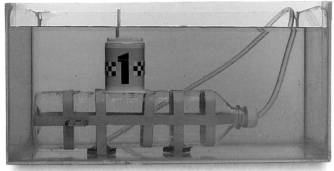

2 Next take out the bottle stoppers and release your grip on the tubing. Water will rush in through the holes in the bottom of the submarine and the vessel will sink.

A real submarine must carry its own supply of air. Because so much is needed, the air has to be made smaller or "compressed" and kept in strong cylinders. Modern submarines can recycle this air, which allows them to stay underwater for up to two years.

Boats have been used for fishing ever since people first built them. As in early times, modern boats are still equipped with hooks, lines and nets, although some have hi-tech computers to help them find the best fishing areas.

MAKE it WORK!

This fishing boat is called a trawler because it uses a funnel-shaped net called a trawl. The net hangs over the back of the boat to catch fish, so it is known as a stern trawler.

You will need

balsa wood	plasticine
a 6-volt flat battery	paper clips
an electric motor	two corks
a plastic seed tray	a hand drill
a plastic netting bag	a brass hook
pliers and a bradawl	thumbtacks
a propeller and shaft	a cotton reel
thick and thin dowel	brass eyelets
wooden and metal beads	electrical wire
ripstop nylon or other cloth	string and glue
copper tubing just wider than the propeller shaft	

1 Block holes in the seed tray with plasticine. Set the motor in a block of plasticine at the front of the boat as shown at the bottom of the page.

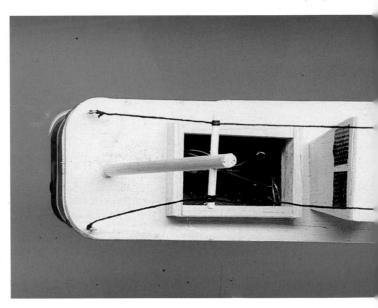

2 Make a hole in the back of the tray with a bradawl. Cut a long and a short piece of copper tubing. Wedge the long tube into the hole and slide the propeller shaft down the tube. Use the shorter tube to connect the shaft with the motor. Secure the join by crimping with pliers. Add paper clips to two wires and connect them to the motor. Now slide the battery under the shaft.

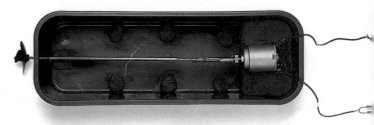

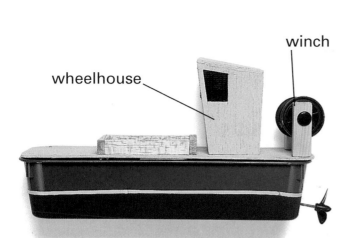

wheelhouse

winch

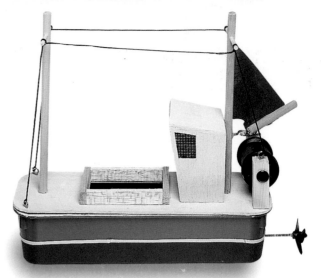

3 Cut the deck out of balsa wood. Cut a large hole directly above the battery as shown on page 36. Glue the deck onto the plastic tray. Make a **wheelhouse** from balsa wood to fit your boat and glue it to the deck.

7 Glue the masts to the deck. Screw eyelets into the deck and winch as shown, and thread with string. Cut a piece of dowel for the boom and join to the mast with a hook and eyelet. Cut out the sail and glue to the mast and boom.

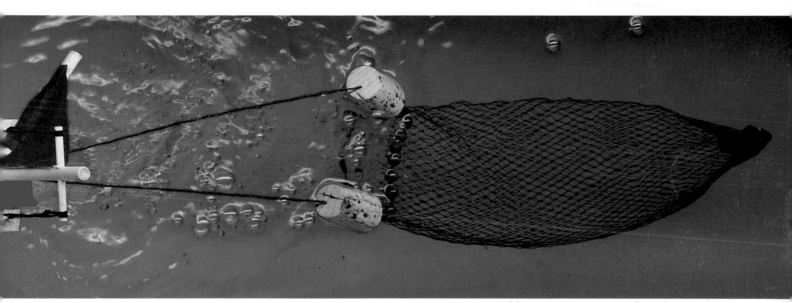

4 Cut four balsa-wood strips to fit around the hole in the deck. Glue them into place.

5 For the **winch**, cut two strips of balsa to hold the cotton reel at the back. Cut a length of dowel just longer than the cotton reel. Slide the dowel through the reel and fix it to the winch supports with drawing pins. Glue the winch to the deck.

6 Make two masts from thick dowel. Drill a hole in each and slide through a piece of thin dowel.

8 For the net, weight the closed end of the netting bag with plasticine. At the open end, thread string with wooden beads through one side and thread metal beads along the other side. Tie two strings to the net, thread a cork onto each and attach the strings to the winch.

Since the earliest days of water travel, carrying cargo has been important. Today, cargo ships carry over 95 per cent of the world's goods. The biggest ships in the world are oil tankers. Some are so huge that the crew need bicycles to get from one end to the other. But big ships are difficult to control and in ports they rely on small, powerful tugs to maneuver them into position.

MAKE it WORK!

The two most important cargo-carrying ships today are oil tankers and container ships. This model can be either a container ship or an oil tanker, depending on the deck design you choose. You can use either model for the loading experiments on pages 40-41.

You will need

glue and screws	paint
thick and thin dowel	plasticine
waterproof tape	a hand drill
eight small corks	balsa wood
$1/10$ in. balsa-wood sheet	a craft knife
a plastic window box and drip tray	

1 Make the window box watertight by sealing the holes with plasticine.

2 Next make the **bridge**, where the crew have their quarters. Cut out the six shapes below left from the sheet of balsa wood. Use the width of the hull to help you work out the sizes.

3 Glue the pieces of the bridge together as shown on the left. Paint the bridge and leave to dry.

4 Shape the funnel from a block of balsa wood and glue to the bridge. Cut a mast from a piece of dowel and drill a hole near the top. Slide in a thin dowel crosspiece. Glue the mast to the bridge.

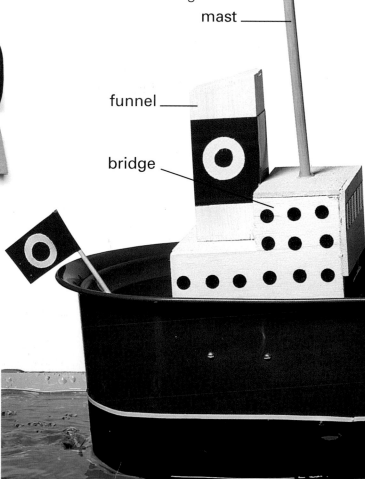

mast

funnel

bridge

5 Make the deck of the ship from the drip tray of the window box. For the oil tanker, mark the position of nine holes in the deck, as shown above. Draw around a cork to make nine circles. Ask an adult to help you cut them out using a craft knife. Press the corks tightly into the holes.

6 For the container ship, cut two rectangular holes in the deck as shown above. Ask an adult to help you do this with a craft knife. You can also add a flag made from thin dowel and tape as shown. Glue the bridge to the deck.

To give your vessel propeller power you will need

balsa wood	a 9-volt flat battery
electrical wire	a bradawl and pliers
a propeller and shaft	paper clips
an electric motor and bracket	
copper tubing just wider than the propeller shaft	

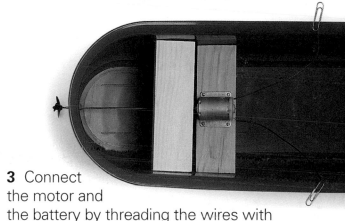

1 Cut two strips of balsa wood to fit across one end of tanker as shown. Glue and screw in place.

2 Screw the motor and bracket to the strip nearest the middle of the boat (the other strip will help to stabilize your vessel). Now follow step 2 on page 36 to join the propeller and motor.

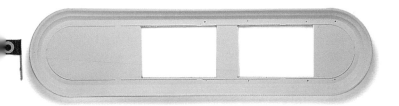

3 Connect the motor and the battery by threading the wires with the paper clips up through the open hole in the tanker deck, or the rectangle in the deck of the container ship. Put the battery in the bridge.

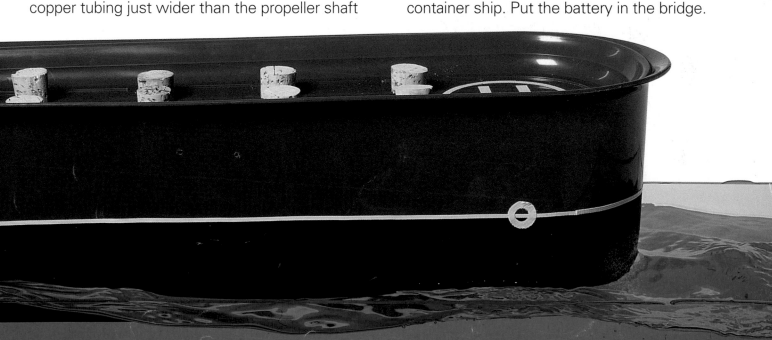

Oil tankers are inexpensive to operate because they need only a small crew and can be unloaded quickly and easily by pumping the oil. But ships carrying tanks of liquid can become unstable unless they are correctly designed.

Oil tanker safety

Every year there are thousands of spills from oil tankers, so shipbuilders are always looking for new ways to improve safety. Tankers today must have a double hull, so that if the outer hull is cracked, the cargo is still intact. The hull should also be split into compartments by divisions called **bulkheads**. This gives the ship greater strength and stability in bad weather and limits leaking.

MAKE it WORK!

This experiment shows you how and why the tanker model from pages 38-39 needs to be adapted if it is going to carry a liquid cargo.

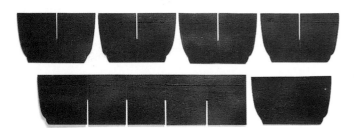

2 Cut out the shapes shown below left from the balsa-wood sheet, making sure that the pieces fit tightly into the hull. Don't make any compartments under the bridge.

3 Slot all the bulkhead pieces together as shown above and insert them in the hull. Then make them watertight by sealing all the edges with plasticine.

You will need
a jug
plasticine
plastic tubing
sheets of balsa wood
a tank or bowl of water
your tanker model, without
  the battery and motor

1 First take the deck off the oil tanker and float the hull in a tank of water. Fill a jug with water and slowly pour it in, as shown above right, to see how easily the ship loses its stability.

4 Now try filling up your boat with liquid once more. Try to balance the boat as you fill it, by pouring a little water into all the compartments first, and then topping up each one.

5 Empty the tanker and put the deck back on. Now try filling the compartments through the holes in the deck by attaching a tube to a squeeze bottle full of water.

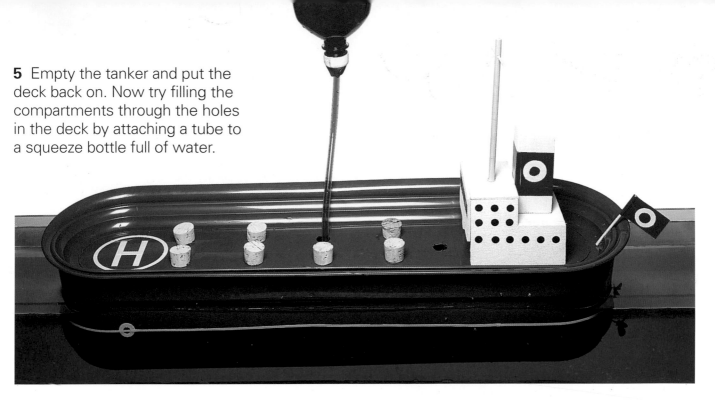

Loading solids

Solid cargoes are often packed onto ships in special units called containers. These containers are the same size the world over, and also fit onto the trailer of a truck.

Make a container ship by using the deck shape below from page 39. Cut some containers from blocks of wood and screw an eyelet into each one, so it can be lifted by a crane.

Making a crane

To make a crane, also known as a **derrick**, cut two pieces of dowel to make a mast and spar. Screw in one eyelet near the bottom of the mast, one at the top, and an eyelet and a hook at either end of the spar. Thread up the strings (shrouds) and attach hooks and eyelets as shown below. Glue the mast to the deck.

When you think of the length of an airport runway it seems incredible that aircraft can take off and land from the deck of a ship in the middle of the ocean. An aircraft carrier flight deck must be flat, relatively stable—even in rough weather—and very big.

You will need

a hand drill	plasticine
brass eyelets	thick and thin dowel
glue and paint	a plastic window box
a yogurt container	tape and rubber bands
cardboard and paper	
$1/10$ and $1/5$ in. sheets of balsa wood	

1 Make the window box watertight with plasticine. Glue 3 strips of $1/10$ in. balsa-wood, 3 x 15 $3/4$ in., edge to edge to make a deck to fit the window box. Add side extensions for the flight deck. Decorate with paint or tape.

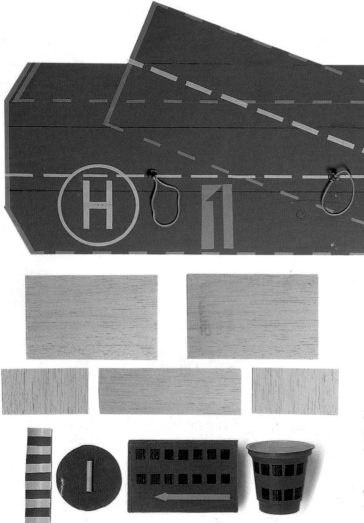

2 Cut five rectangles of $1/5$ in. thick balsa wood as shown at left. Choose a size to fit your window box. Glue together to make the bridge.

3 Cut a balsa-wood lid for the yogurt container and glue it on to make a control tower. Glue the control tower to the bridge and the bridge to the deck.

4 To make a mast, drill a hole near the top of the thick dowel. Slide in a crosspiece of thin dowel. Make a radar aerial from dowel and a rectangle of cardboard. Glue the mast and aerial to the bridge. Fasten the rubber bands to the eyelets and screw them into the deck in the positions shown above.

MAKE it WORK!

Modern aircraft carriers have computer-controlled stabilizers to keep the boat steady. They also have catapults to give aircraft extra speed at take-off, and arrester wires to help them stop on landing. This model has a catapult system for launching paper planes.

5 The carrier is now complete. Add some paper planes, as shown on the next page.

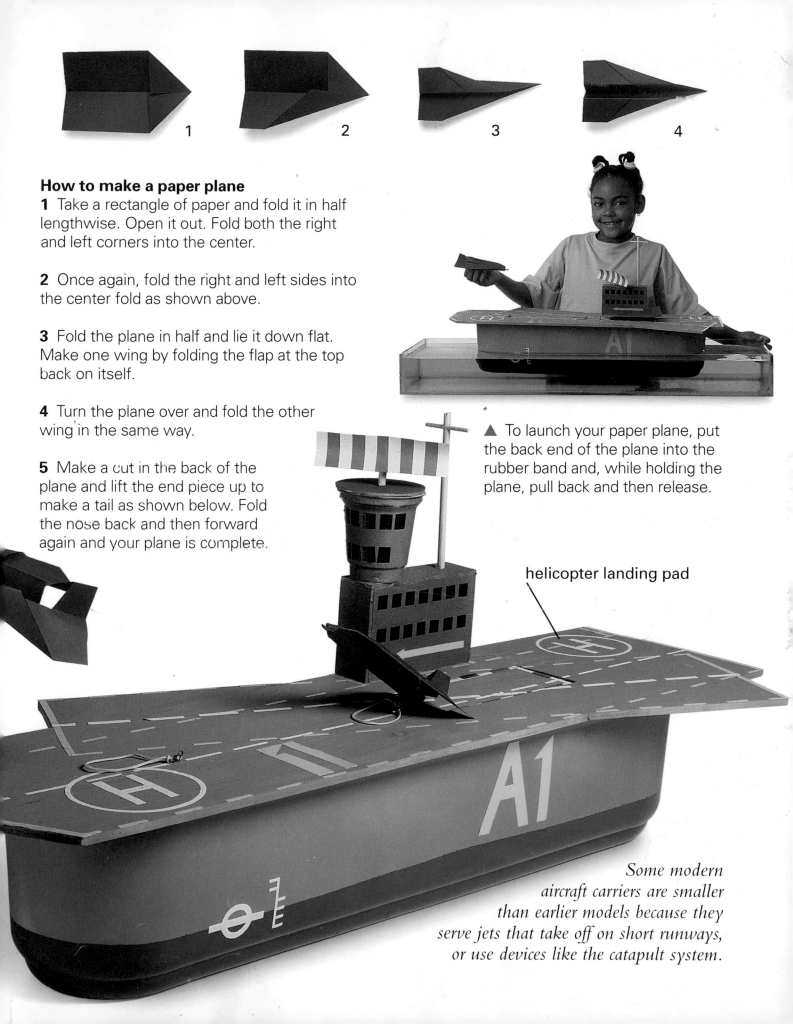

1   **2**   **3**   **4**

How to make a paper plane

1 Take a rectangle of paper and fold it in half lengthwise. Open it out. Fold both the right and left corners into the center.

2 Once again, fold the right and left sides into the center fold as shown above.

3 Fold the plane in half and lie it down flat. Make one wing by folding the flap at the top back on itself.

4 Turn the plane over and fold the other wing in the same way.

5 Make a cut in the back of the plane and lift the end piece up to make a tail as shown below. Fold the nose back and then forward again and your plane is complete.

▲ To launch your paper plane, put the back end of the plane into the rubber band and, while holding the plane, pull back and then release.

helicopter landing pad

Some modern aircraft carriers are smaller than earlier models because they serve jets that take off on short runways, or use devices like the catapult system.

The silting-up of harbors and important shipping routes on rivers is a problem in many parts of the world. Dredgers keep busy harbors and shipping channels open by scooping mud and silt from the river or seabed and depositing it elsewhere.

MAKE it WORK!

A bucket dredger uses a string of buckets on a conveyor belt to bring mud up from the bottom. This bucket dredger has a flat bottom so that it can navigate silted-up river channels.

You will need

paint	burlap
plastic pipe	a hand drill
$1/5$ in. dowel	thumbtacks
10 small yogurt containers	glue and tape
$1/3$ in. and $2/5$ in. thick balsa wood	

1 Cut out the pieces of balsa wood for a hull $11^4/5$ in. long and $4^3/4$ in. wide, but check the boat is wide enough for the yogurt containers. Paint and leave to dry. Drill two holes in the sides at the back, to fit the dowel. Glue together the pieces of the hull as shown below. Do not insert the dowel yet.

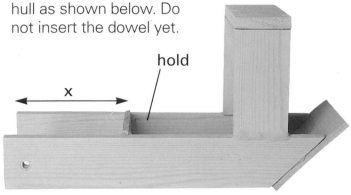

It is very important that the back of the boat, marked **x** above, is long enough. You should be able to fit a piece of pipe and a yogurt container in it. Then allow at least $1/2$ in. between the container and the back of the **hold**.

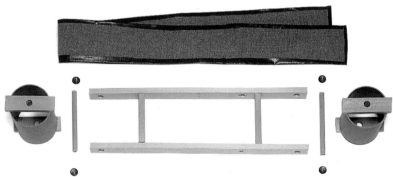

2 For the conveyor belt, make a ladder 11 in. long and 3 in. wide from $1/3$ in. balsa strips. Drill six holes in the sides, big enough to fit the pieces of dowel, as above. Glue ladder together.

3 Cut two pieces of pipe to fit just inside the ends of the ladder. Cut four rectangles of balsa wood just wider than the diameter of the pipes, and drill a hole in each. Glue the wood rectangles to the pipe as shown above.

4 Cut two dowels to go through the pipes and fasten the pipes to the ladder using thumbtacks. Cut a piece of burlap to go around the frame. Tape the edges to prevent fraying.

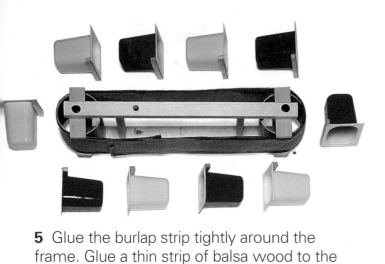

7 Push the dowel at the back of the dredger through both the hull and the ladder frame. It should be a tight fit. Glue the ends of the dowel into the hull, but don't glue the dowel to the ladder frame.

5 Glue the burlap strip tightly around the frame. Glue a thin strip of balsa wood to the lip of each yogurt container.

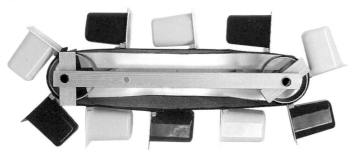

6 Glue the containers, all facing the same way and equally spaced, onto the burlap as shown.

8 Your dredger is now ready to try out in a tank of water with some gravel or sand in the bottom. You can adjust the angle of the conveyor belt so that it just reaches the gravel on the bottom. Move the conveyor belt by pulling on the buckets above the water line.

Ballast The extra weight added to a hull to give it stability or to make it float evenly.

Bermuda rig The sail arrangement used on most modern sailing boats, with a triangular mainsail set on a tall mast.

Bow The forward part of a hull.

Bowsprit A pole that sticks out from the front of a boat, and to which the jib sails are set.

Bridge The raised area on a ship from which it is navigated or steered.

Bulkheads Partitions within the hull of a vessel, that divide it into watertight compartments and give added strength.

Canoe A small, narrow open boat that can either be paddled or sailed.

Catamaran A sailing boat with two narrow hulls connected together by the deck.

Centerboard A wooden or metal plate that can be raised or lowered to allow a shallow-hulled boat to sail in different depths of water.

Coracle A small, light, rounded boat made from a wooden frame covered with canvas or skin. Similar boats are still used for river transport and fishing in some parts of the world.

Cutter A single-masted sailing vessel with a mainsail set from a gaff, a topsail set above, and two jibs set to a bowsprit.

Density The weight of a material in relation to its volume. For example, a coin made of lead weighs more than a coin of the same size made of plastic. This is because lead has a higher density.

Derrick A large pole or spar fixed at its base to a mast with a system of ropes and pulleys and used on board ship as a crane for unloading and loading cargo.

Dhow A cargo vessel with a lateen rig. Dhows are used for trading in the Red Sea, the Persian Gulf and the Indian Ocean.

Energy When something has energy it can make things move, change shape or warm up. For example, food gives people energy; fuel, such as petrol, gives energy to vessels.

Engine A machine that burns fuel to provide it with power.

Fore and aft Running along a line from the front of the vessel to the back. In a fore-and-aft rig, the sails are set on either side of the mast along the line of the hull.

Forestay A rope or cable supporting the front mast of a sailing vessel, running from the top of the mast to the bow or end of the bowsprit.

Gaff A pole or spar in a fore-and-aft rig from which a mainsail is set.

Halyard A rope or wire used to hoist and lower a sail.

Hold The space in a vessel for storing cargo.

Hull The main body of a vessel, the part that floats on the water.

Jib A triangular sail used by sailing vessels set on rigging called stays at the bow.

Keel A long, strong wooden or steel girder running along the bottom of a hull, to which hull frames are fastened. In some sailing vessels the keel is extended into a fin sticking out below the main hull.

Lateen rig A tall, narrow triangular sail fastened to a long pole or spar that is set fore and aft at an angle on the mast.

Main sheet A rope used to trim the mainsail by tightening or loosening it to make best use of the wind.

Mainsail The largest sail on a sailing vessel. The mainsail is usually the lowest sail on the main mast.

Outrigger A log of wood fastened on long poles to the side of a dugout canoe, to make the boat more stable at sea when paddled or under sail.

Rig The arrangement of masts and sails on a sailing vessel.

Rudder A large board fastened to the back or stern of a boat below the water. The rudder is mounted on "hinges" and can be moved from side to side to steer the vessel.

Shroud A rope or cable used to support the mast of a sailing vessel from the sides.

Single scull A small, light rowboat used for racing and rowed by one person.

Spar A wooden or metal pole used to support a sail in some way. Booms, yards, gaffs and bowsprits are all types of spar.

Stern The rear part of a hull.

Tacking A means of traveling a course that goes directly against the wind by sailing diagonally into the wind in a series of zigzags, or tacks.

Thrust The pushing power, that a propeller gives to a boat.

Tiller A long handle that is connected to the top of the rudder on a small boat, and used for steering a vessel by hand.

Wheelhouse An enclosed cabin on the deck of a vessel that houses the wheel used for steering it.

Winch A drum or cylinder powered by a motor or by hand and used to haul in or let out a rope or cable.

Yacht Any kind of sailing boat used for sport or pleasure rather than for carrying cargo or passengers.

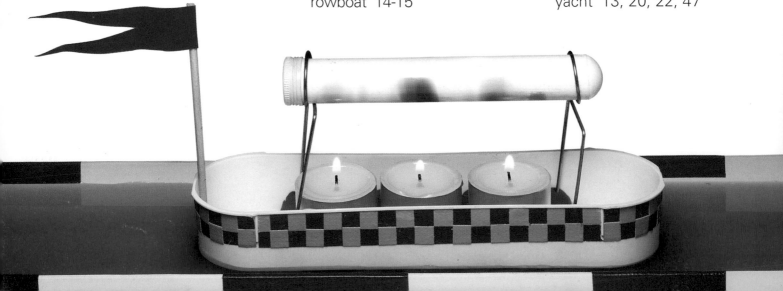